Living...

Davon Ansley

DAVON'S WORLD

Published by Davon's World
Dade City, Florida

Printed in the United States of America
First Paperback Edition - May 2024

Paperback ISBN: 979-8-218-41963-9

Edited by: Khloe's Thoughts Editing
Cover by: Make Your Mark Publishing Solutions
Layout by: Make Your Mark Publishing Solutions

CONTENTS

ENERGY

NEGATIVITY

We're told not to judge others, but we do instead.
I believe that we shouldn't live in the past,
Even though a lot of us constantly think about
How simple it was back in those days compared to now.
The way things are today makes me question.
Are we going forward or backward.
Anger is everywhere and it seems like there's no
escaping it.
Even in the comfort of your own home.
This is how many live
Day to day, mad.
Some may be lost and confused, don't know where to go.
Just maybe they will find their true selves, just maybe.

WASTING TIME

You've put your all into something only to get nowhere.
It's like you took one step forward just to get pushed two
steps back.
All the hopes and dreams you had are now gone.
Disappointment is all within you,
After this, you don't know what else you can do.
Things are not going to always go our way.
And setbacks like this proves that.
Others around you try to pick you up out of your funk.
Even though they mean good, they just don't fully know.
Defeat starts to get the best of you.
You may want to be alone however long it takes you.
The day seem like it just drags on longer and longer.
As nothing appears to make you satisfied.

WHEN DEPRESSION TAKES OVER

I think it's safe to say
That we all have been through some sort of depression.
We want to be isolated from others.
There are many reasons why we get like this.
While being alone it's kind of hard to think good
When a bunch of negativity is around us.
Talking to friends or family could be easy.
But some may not fully understand.
Emptiness is how the day starts.
Not knowing where to go or say is the norm.
Whenever we get out of that dark spot
And began to talk about what's wrong.
We become relieved of the heavy burden we carry around.
It may not be easy but all we have to do is talk.
Say what's on our mind, honestly.

SAVING GRACE

Having good people in our lives
Are some of the best things that are offered to us for free.
What we should do is release all the turmoil on the
inside out
And leave it there for good.
Because we all have those moments
Where we're not at our best and it can get to us.
It is up to us to decide how we end things.
On a good note, or bad note.
But getting past them
To become a stronger person is what we all should be
striving for.
It's good to have a listening ear for someone to go to
When we need it the most.
Trying our best not to judge and to hear them out.
That person thanks you for being there, not everybody is
able to do that.

FRESH START

A new chance is waiting for you.
Getting a new opportunity to do something over again.
Might not seem too bad after all.
You weren't ready the first time.
But this time you are going to do better than you did before.
Not spending too much time on the past
Because you have something ahead of you to focus on.
You shouldn't be nervous; you don't want to repeat the same mistake.
Who knows, this may be the last time.
Stay calm and confident and watch what happens.

CHOOSING TO SMILE

None of us should live in a make-believe world.
Pretending like we're so perfect.
No matter where we're at
There still is something that we could improve on
Or wish for something else to transpire.
But even through all of that
We could go through situations being happy.
Nothing should be so painful to where you're so distressed.
That you don't have a little hope for what's next.
Who knows? What's next could be the big breakthrough
that you may want.
Going through this thing called life with hope will get us
through.
Keeping our head up more than down so we can see where
we're going next.

COURAGEOUS

It takes a brave person to try a new solution.
Being the type to go left when everybody is going right.
We get stuck in doing the same thing over and over again.
We can get complacent about how we go about things.
Being the first in whatever group you're in might be scary
at first.
More than likely, you're going to make mistakes.
But if you know what you do is good,
And you stick to making that very thing come into fruition.
Everything will come at the right time.
People will question you because they want to know how
you did it.
So that they can have the same amount of boldness
you got.
Don't get offended by them, tell them so they could be
inspired too.

THINK BIG

I remember seeing posts about having dreams.
It can be so simple yet still useful for many to use.
Posts about having dreams that are daring.
And how if your dreams are not scaring you then it may
not be for you.
Many times, we don't want to go for something that we
think is out of our reach.
I know within certain demographics and different areas of
the world,
They have different ways of doing things.
Some may call it small minded and if I'm being honest,
Small minded is probably the correct way to explain it.
Thinking outside the box can be good when aiming for
something.
Not just with some people but all areas of the world.
Breaking all boundaries and going for what you want.
You can do a lot of things if you put your mind to it.
There's only one you, so why not try to push what you
know to the fullest limit.

IT'S EASY TO...

It's easy to have envy against other people.
Rather than congratulate them when they have achieved greatness.
It's easy to complain about everything.
Rather than taking the good with the bad.
It's easy to talk down on someone.
Rather than giving them a compliment or not saying anything at all.
It's easy to get mad very easily before fully understanding a situation.
Rather than staying calm even when things don't turn out good.
It's easy to choose violence first.
Rather than handling conflict like mature human beings.
We shouldn't be ashamed because we all have done one or many of these.
Just think if we all were to go about things in a more relaxed manner.
How different the world may be, just think.

STAY GROUNDED

Not staying so focused on the past but remembering where
we started at
Is something we shouldn't ever forget.
It is what keeps us gracious and levelheaded.
So many times, when people get to a certain level.
They want to get on a high horse that they think they can't
come down off.
It's like they lose a part of themselves for something that
isn't promised.
Having accomplishments shouldn't define who we are.
It's good to be a hard worker that receives recognition.
It's also good to stay aware of our behavior,
Being thoughtful of the way we treat others
When they may not have what we have.
There's nothing wrong with celebrating our wins.
But also know that with every win comes new hurdles.

YOUTH

ENJOY THE MOMENTS

It's so amazing how a young person
Can get the chance to live out everything they can.
Prom nights are a big thing.
Just like senior pictures that will stay with them for the rest
of their lives.
Experience being in a relationship that they probably will
regret later on.
Walking across the graduation stage
And it finally hits them that they're not a child anymore.
Whatever pathway they go it's now a reflection of them.
Not being in a rush to being an adult.
Soaking up this stage in life is significant
Because the real test is upon them.

PARENTS DO UNDERSTAND

It's an old expression, something that many teens have felt.
Whenever they don't see eye to eye with their parents.
They want to hang out with their friends on a late night.
And the parents say no.
Comments are said underneath the child's breath.
They huff and puff so hard that they can blow the house down.
But all in actuality the parent is looking out for their child.
No parent in their right mind
Don't want to see their child in a place where they're in harm's way.
A lot of times the parents have been there.
And saw how things went for them or others around them.
By telling their child no,
They're protecting them from going down a path they may know.
Because their path wasn't as good as their child has it.
Parents tell their children no because it's their instinct.
That child probably can't stand their parents right now,
But in the future, they will hopefully thank them.

FOR THE GIRLS

Girls that are evolving into young women.
I know you're getting a lot of attention.
Because many of the girls I grew up with got it too.
Your body is growing.
When you walk somewhere, all eyes be on you.
Many males would love to be with you.
They give compliments to get some of your attention.
You may smile at them, not trying to hurt their feelings.
You may not know your power.
But if you do then you know the game that has been taught
to you.
Stay motivated to do what's right.
Even if that means not having that many people
around you.
You stand for what you have been taught.
Don't try to follow the hype.
That may get you caught in something you don't want any
parts of.
This is strictly for the princesses that one day will become
queens.

TEEN PARENT

It's the moment that every parent doesn't want to believe.
Their baby is having a baby and don't know what to do next.
It's unexpected, even if you told your child multiple times.
The consequences of having unprotected sex.
Many do what they want to do.
For the young girl, all thoughts are running through your head.
One of those thoughts is how scary it's going to be.
Another thought is how are you going to get through this?
Will the boy be around to help? Is another question.
For the young boy, you're scared too.
That's the reason why many run away from being a dad.
You're not the one that's carrying the baby.
So, you don't have to feel all of the different emotions of having a baby.
You love your girl but something you felt was so good is so real.
As her belly grows with a new human being on its way.
The time is soon near another statistic is what they say,
But a new bundle of joy is what the family has.

IT'S GOING TO BE OK

For the kids that have no other choice
But to walk alone while others tease them, this is for
you all.
I know the shame you go through with constantly
questioning yourself.
Pondering on your self-worth
And how others are supposedly better than you.
But newsflash they're not, no matter how low a person's
self-esteem is.
We all have something that we're not too proud of.
People can bully and pick on whoever.
Just to cover up their true views on themselves.
That one finger that's pointing at someone.
Has three others pointing back at them.
So, to the kids that are considered the outcast
It's alright to walk alone for a little bit.
This don't have to be your end.

WELCOME TO THE REAL WORLD

Coming out of high school is typically a big deal for most.
Entering the world as a young adult can be exciting.
Once people reach a certain age
It seems as if nobody can tell them anything.
Because in their eyes they grown, which technically
they are.
The true adulthood will come into full force.
Once they were no longer in their parent's house and in
their own.
It's a time to experiment without having too much of a
guardian.
It's a fun time but also a lot of learning and growing up
time, for some.
Teaching oneself about how to survive by themselves.
In a world that can be cruel is something
That should make anyone that doesn't crumble stronger.
Being brave enough to fully understand.
The ways of not cracking down when under pressure
Is one of the many things that helps thicken our skin.
Even toward the latter part of life.

NOT REALLY THAT BAD

Becoming a grown person with responsibilities can be a lot at first.

It's the moment that a lot of us wait for but when it happens.

Many wish they were back at home with their parents.

It seems like every time you pick your head up.

Something is coming to you with a due date.

Looking back over a person's childhood, depending on how they grew up.

May not seem as stressful as it was.

Yeah, it wasn't fun being told what to do, when to do it, and how to do it.

The good thing about this stage is now the ball is in your court

You get to completely make your own decisions.

Even though most things that we come to terms with

Have its pros and cons.

COMING OF AGE

We don't get to have young love for too long.
But during that stage we get to know who we are and what we like.
It's rare to see someone with their high school sweetheart at an older age.
When you're young you think that the person, you're in love with
Is going to be with you forever.
The good and bad of a relationship is shown.
And it's up to the individuals that are in that.
To choose to go on with whatever they think is best for them.
Wild party nights and early morning hangovers tend to be the norm.
But they're young so they pretend to shake it off as they head onto start their day.
They are not fully aware of their behavior.
Some are but choose not to do anything about it.
Because most people around them are doing the same thing.
For the ones that have parents, they're nervous about their child's actions.
It doesn't matter how much they get talked to
They are still going to do what they think is cool while they're young.

EARLY TWENTIES

When a pretty young woman walks into a room men stare in amazement.
The older men that haven't had a young woman on their arms in a while.
Starts to fantasize about how it was for them when they were that age.
Women that dress a certain kind of way are constantly complimented.
They have grown into their grown woman body.
And the men lose their mind every time she walks by them.
Skin be so soft and glistening as the sun hits them.
Clothes that hug their bodies so they can show off their figure.
Men are also admired at this age, but not like the women.
Hip hop songs are made about young people.
In particular, women that fit the image the rappers rap about.
Young men and women have their whole life ahead of them.
Even though people around this age are good looking.
They're more than just looks.
The future is in their hands.
And it's going to take more than having good looks to be a conqueror.

FIGURING IT OUT

There are some things that are given to us freely.
However, some things are an on-going mission.
To open our minds to something else
Rather it be love, friendships, or other typical subjects that many people face.
When we're in our twenties it's expected for us not to have all of the answers.
We get mad, frustrated, and some even want to take their anger out on people.
Even after that the problem is still facing us.
In our minds, the question is asked, what are you going to do?
How about be still for a moment and allow signs to appear to tell you what to do.
We can get so busy especially with allowing thoughts to overflow our heads.
That it's hard for us to stay quiet and free our minds to receive the solution.
When you're young, so is your body.
And all the fast movement can wear any of us out.
Moving around so much can be distracting us from whatever it is.
But we all get tired and are going to need a break.
So no, we're not going to have everything figured out in our time.
It's ok to be unsure and sit still to hopefully find that glimmer of hope.

LIFE

SPECIAL DELIVERY

Holding a baby for the first time is something that many
parents remember.
The soft skin, the big expressive eyes, and the cute little
movements they do
Are just a few things that will attach parents to their
little one.
It is hard for them to stay far away from them,
Thinking about what their baby is doing.
Watching them sleep so peacefully as they lay innocently
in their baby cribs.
Even with all the crying and sleepless nights
A parent wouldn't trade it for anything in the world.
A small, defenseless human being depends on you for
everything.
When they become a toddler, they kind of start doing
things on their own.
But they still look and sometimes cry to you for help.
One of the best gifts in the world
Is having a child that you love dearly.

GROWING UP AS A KID

Eighteen years is the typical amount of time for a child to grow.
There are many changes that kids experience.
While in elementary they can start off a little shy
By not knowing exactly how important those first few years of school are.
Kids go from learning in the classroom to playing in recess.
They may have crushes, but many don't act on it.
Middle school is a bit different, most of their bodies start to change.
It's kind of like, for lack of better words,
That awkward stage that most kids go through.
Hanging out with friends that could go into being life-long friends.
Having crushes and possibly hanging out with them.
By the time they get to high school many put themselves into groups.
Puppy love is all in the air for many.
As teens get closer to adulthood
Those last memories of being a child are special.
The parents get a little emotional
As they watch their child grow to being their own individuals.

NEVER STOP LEARNING

It doesn't matter how old we get learning should be a part of us.

We should never get to a point where we think we know everything.

And no one could tell us anything because that's not true.

When we not only listen but take what we learned

And apply it to something, we can take something out of that.

By teaching others what we learned

That news could go on and on to others that may need to hear it.

Not being so selfish

To where we're not open to hearing other possibilities.

None of us on this earth are perfect and we shouldn't act like we are.

We do know what we know but that's not everything.

Growing is not just considered for height but for our day-to-day life.

THANKFUL

Waking up to seeing another day should never be taken for granted.

Having a home to safely sleep in everyday is something to appreciate.

To have the strength to put on clean clothes and shoes must be a good feeling.

Being able to go into your own kitchen to have meals to eat should have us smiling.

Going through the normal activities such as working, driving your own vehicle,

And other things can be looked at as small but great to have.

Something else great to have is taking the time out.

To realize that we may not be where we want.

But the little things that we have are just as significant as the other things.

No matter how far we go, we shouldn't get too comfortable.

To where we forget to recognize what we have.

We never know if those same things will be there tomorrow.

1 THING EVERYBODY HAS IN COMMON

Mistakes are something that we all are going to make.
Rather we learn from them is up to us.
From a baby until now
We all have done some wrongdoings.
Just because we do something that isn't good
Doesn't make us bad people.
It's the lesson in making bad decisions
That gets us into unfair results.
So, it doesn't matter about your race, gender, age,
Or any other groupings
Mistakes will be made throughout this thing called life.
Once you fall, don't stay there crying about it for too long.
Dust yourself off, observe what you did,
And know not to do that again.
If you are going to try it over
Make some adjustments.
Stay with a willing mind to know what's right and wrong.

UNFAIR

We all have those times where we think our back is against the wall.
The situation that we're in seems as if it couldn't get any worse.
There are sleepless nights, crying becomes the norm, and so many other things.
Friends and family tell you that it will be ok.
But for some, they may not fully understand what's going on.
Rather it be you don't tell people everything due to embarrassment or other reasons.
The problem is still there and after a while.
When we don't know what's going to happen next.
The unexpected happen and the dark days seem like they're coming to an end.
No more hurt because we've hurt for too long.
That is one of the times that something happens.
To show us that we can have it a little tough with certain situations.

SIGNS WE'RE GIVEN

Somethings are told to us without having a single word said.
The way a person acts toward us says a lot.
And how we allow them to treat us speaks even more.
Who wants people around that are not for them?
I know for me being an observant more than a talker
There have been many times where I have been shown to back away from others.
They're not good for me even though I have been good to them.
I'm no angel; I just continue to learn who people are as time goes on.
Finding sincere people seems hard to find nowadays.
There's so much evilness
That it can be difficult to know who's genuinely being a good person.
Not only are good people can be hard to come by
But knowing what's good for you can be questionable.
Hints for us sometimes are right in our faces.
At these times we must pay attention to what's around us.
When we do that, it should make us more aware and less naïve.
So that the next time we will know how to block out the madness.

LETTING GO

Not every person is going to be with us forever.
If we're hardheaded then we may have to be taught
something repeatedly.
Learning that everybody is not for us can be a hard pill to
swallow.
Even when we know it's bad and choose to still go on with
it like it's not that bad.
It can leave us with an unpleasant surprise.
Choosing to distance yourself from someone is one thing.
The reason being is that we can still go to that same person
again.
But when we choose to permanently remove ourselves
It takes bravery, not everyone is going to let something go.
But for those who chose to, for their good.
Good for you, you shouldn't allow something to bring you
down.
To where you forget about your integrity.
Walking away from a situation to better your peace is
commendable.
A peace of mind is better than no mind.

GETTING OLD

This is not to offend anyone.
It's a good thing to see the second half of life.
Everyone can't say that.
But for those that can be grateful
You made it so far and you're not done yet.
So, what if you have grey hair
Or you don't move as fast as the younger people do,
You're still here and you made it.
You should be filled with wisdom
And experience to tell others around you.
So don't be afraid of the years passing by
And you start to dread things more as time goes on.
You're still needed,
Even when they tell you you're not,
You all are acknowledged.

DEATH

It's very hard to accept when someone has died.
You're in disbelief; the person you love so much is no
longer here.
For you to hug them, kiss them, and tell them what's on
your mind.
You question yourself, like what could I have done to make
them stay?
When the phone calls stop and you're no longer receiving
text messages
From others to console you because time has passed on.
That person is still on your mind.
No matter what you do, no matter where you go
Images of that person continue to run through your head.
One day, you pulled yourself up and dried away the tears.
The memories are still there and won't ever go away.
You found that there is life for you after losing someone.

CHALLENGES

THE UNEXPECTED

It happens to us all.

Something bad comes to us without any warning.

Many are confused and normally we'll get upset.

Some take things that are thrown at us as a test to see how strong we are.

Those are the ones that don't mind telling others what they have been through.

Life is full of curveballs that it doesn't matter how we try to escape it.

The issue at hand is still there.

Some will crumble,

In hopes of somebody coming to rescue them.

Easily being fooled by the unexpected

However, there are many that will stand tall.

Even when there's no answer in sight.

My question to you is, which one are you?

SELF-DOUBT

It could be a generational curse.
That has you thinking you're not good enough.
Maybe you were told by someone that you wouldn't
amount to nothing.
Or comments in your head constantly plays over.
About the terrible things that were said to you.
Your dreams have been shattered.
Right along with your confidence.
You see other people being content with themselves.
And you ask yourself, why not me?
It can be difficult to stop belittling yourself when that's all
you know.
It's easier said than done to stop the bad habits.
But ask yourself this, are you going to allow everything
great past you by?
Letting your past stay in your present
Getting used to the same ole same ole with your future.
People gone say and do what they want.
That's why you should surround yourself with good people,
And those good vibes will hopefully rub off on you.

HARSH REALITY

You try to stop thinking about what's going on.
You don't want to expect something that isn't easy to accept.
We all make mistakes and this one you made seems to get the best of you.
Somehow, you have acknowledged your mistakes, made your sincere apologies,
And you wait for the outcome.
You're still kind of in disbelief.
That something you did could cause a big complication.
You try not to allow fear to take control of you.
Because if you allow it then you could possibly redo what you did wrong.
After this experience you will learn to never do it again.
You have accepted things for what it is.
You're moving on in stride.

BLACK WOMEN

To all of the Black Queens out there I have a message
for you.
I apologize for the way society has been to you.
Yes, you are some of the most smartest,
Beautiful and strong individuals this world has ever seen.
You have been mistreated and left to defend yourself.
Even though you have gone through so much pain,
It's time to uplift you in the best way possible.
I can only do so much, but while I'm here.
I can give you your flowers with these words I put together.
When they tell you you're not worth anything,
You are worth more than they know.
Leave that person, they don't deserve to be in your
presence.
You know who you are and don't need those silly types of
validations.
To all the Black Queens that's reading this, you're amazing.

UNWELCOME HOME

We have come so far from family love.
These times we not only have anger in the streets,
But also, in the homes of families.
There was a time when people could come home and be
safe.
Safe from the evilness that's around them.
There would be cooked meals with a table prepared for a
family to sit at.
Nowadays hardly anyone is sitting at the table and eating
together.
Nobody wants to talk to each other.
They are too busy watching TV and, on their phones,
talking to others.
It seems as if people enjoy their friends more than they do
their own family.
When a family does talk with each other it's like no
compassion is there.
The only time a lot of families come together is during
funerals.
Stories being told and tears being shed as they miss their
loved one.
It doesn't have to be a funeral to bring a family together.
We don't have to be the most lovey-dovey people,
But it doesn't take much to tell people you love them,
To bring a family that has been broken apart together.

SO STUBBORN

We all have acted as if we're the only person that matters.
Saying things before we think just to get under someone's
skin to bother them.
Some people are like that and see nothing wrong with it.
It's alarming how people can get so full of themselves.
As if they're the only person in the world.
Not being grateful,
Having a tone of voice that is used to hurt than help.
Rewarding bad behavior seems to be ok.
Not just with children but adults too.
I too get frustrated about the responses of others.
But I try not to let the behaviors of some upset me.
To the point that I completely become one of them.
None of us should allow the bullheadedness of others to get
to us.
Because just like a boomerang,
What you do to others will be done to you.

MISERY LOVES COMPANY

You can very well become the people you hang around.
If somebody is always talking badly about someone
around you.
Nine times out of ten they talk badly about you.
It's one thing to dwell on something for one moment,
But if a person is constantly being a Debbie Downer
And you tried to stop them from being like that.
But they just keep on being like that around you
It's time to leave them alone,
Atleast until they become more pleasant to be around.
Not everyone that you come across is going to be there
for you.
Figuring that out can be the hard part for some.
For those that stand firm in what they believe.
You don't have a problem with cutting someone off for your
well-being.
I commend you, who wants to have a bunch of negativity
around them.
Keep those good relationships near and dear to you.
A person is supposed to encourage and help you, never to
bring distress.

IS IT WORTH IT?

Is it worth talking down on someone just to bring
yourself up?
Is it worth being a bully just to prove your dominance?
Is it worth jumping to conclusions when you don't know all
the facts?
These questions are hopefully left
With answers that could be applied to whomever.
Typically, when someone doesn't get their way.
Or something is done to them that they don't agree with
They typically get this hostility about them.
Words are said and actions are done sometimes in a
bad way.
Even after all of that, you should ask yourself,
What you did or said, was the solution worth it?
When we don't change because we think too much of
ourselves
Things will happen to us to show us
That none of what we did was worth it.

FORGIVE YOURSELF

You have been put down for too long, it's time to pick yourself up.
None of what you went through was justifiable.
Even if they don't apologize to you, forgive yourself.
Forgive yourself for allowing someone to play you.
Forgive yourself for not knowing your own worth.
Forgive yourself for being a doormat to be walked all over.
Forgive yourself for thinking that things were right,
Knowing that they were wrong.
Forgive yourself because you don't want to repeat none of this again.
Males and females shouldn't be ok with being tolerated.
No human being with morals should be tolerated, they should be cared for.
Rather in love, friendships, family, jobs, households etc.
We all should be treated fairly and when we're not, let that person go.
It can be difficult at first, but after a while you will thank yourself.

A DOSE OF KARMA

They have gone through enough time with being evil.
Allowing bad thoughts to get in their head and acting on it.
So now they're receiving all the badness they put out there
on them.
It happened out of nowhere,
They thought they were up with their heads in the cloud.
And now they've been brought down to a snake's level.
Shocked at how things turned out for them.
If they have a heart, they should be thinking about the type
of person they are.
How they somehow found enjoyment in making other lives
miserable.
They want others to feel for them.
But it's kind of hard when they been nothing but the
bad guy.
Yes, we should be thoughtful to others.
Laughing at people, with bad intentions, should never be
the case.
It's just when karma comes back on people.
Stand back so that you won't get any of it on you.

CHANGES

REACTIONS TO CHANGE

From the richest of the rich to the poorest of the poor.
Everybody will experience some type of change.
It's our response to something not being
The way it used to be that differs.
Change can be good for us depending on the situation.
It could lead us to happiness, peace and all the answers
we're looking for.
Then you have the difficult adjustments that we come
across
That makes us wonder, what did we do wrong?
Some go to the extreme with rage filling them.
Seeking any excuse to take their aggravation out on others.
Some just roll with the punches.
Not allowing something to get them excited
About an ordeal they can't change.
Besides whom wants to live in a world
Where everything is always the same?

NEW DAY

Yesterday is gone, you may have gone through some rough moments.
But you woke up to see another day, to make this one better.
Who knows what this day may bring?
It may go better than any other day.
Having you laugh at a lot.
And open your eyes to something else you may not have noticed before.
It could also be another day that seems to lag on
Wishing you can start the day over again.
The morning time can be taken for granted.
Many people spend the morning cranky, not wanting to be around people.
The start of a day is more than likely how we're going to spend the rest of the day.
We shouldn't allow yesterday's worries to stop today's possibilities.

SOMETHING DIFFERENT

Before getting mad, they tell us to count to ten or take a deep breath.

But does that really work in the time of craziness.

Many of us are so used to our unreasonable behavior.

That we get stuck with reacting illogically.

I do believe that things happen to us as a test.

A test to see how long it will take for us to see our ways are not the best.

Yelling, getting mad easily, even going as far as using profanity language

Are some actions that we may do to let out those vile actions.

When we let it out it's usually on others.

However, do we ever stop to think about others or the circumstances?

Understanding our actions can be a bit too much.

We want to get our point across

But should try to be a little considerate before we jump to conclusion.

SCENERY

Having that special place to go to can be crucial in making wise choices.
Rather it be standing by a beautiful beach taking in the air for an hour.
Or going somewhere else that brings you calmness.
Sometimes we do have to get out of the house for a little while
And see things that aren't in our home.
As a home body, taking those walks or drives to places
To get the mind right is good for us.
So, when you think nothing is going your way
And you just want to get outside just for a moment.
Go somewhere, preferably by yourself and enjoy the outside views.
Focus on serenity and bring that back with you.
As you come back to the place you left
Whatever you went through is now behind you.

SELF-LOST

A lot of people start from the bottom, and they make their rise to the top.
Some act gracious by not allowing things to get to their head.
As for those that become arrogant, by being filled with pride.
About what they have and forget how they were before they made it.
In the long run, you're hurting only yourself.
To prove yourself,
You think of bringing others down to make it seem as if you're so big and bad.
They're not bad at all, they just lost themselves.
Hopefully, they are able to find a clue soon before they start to lose more.
It's unfortunate that things can change people for the worse.
Starting off humble and heading into corruption.
We must remember this one thing,
As quickly as we get something, we can lose it all in the snap of a finger.

FOR A SEASON

I wrote about how people change when they get up in life.
Now this time, I'm writing about how we change,
But the people around us don't.
A long time ago, it was told to me that
Once you start doing good not everyone around you is
going to be proud of you.
Some people are so low that they will wish for your
downfall.
Secretly holding hate and envy for what you're doing.
To make a long story short, not everybody is your friend.
Not everybody is meant to be in your life forever.
Those cheers that they give can be fake.
So, when somebody leaves you and shows you who they
are once
Believe them, there's nothing to try to rekindle.
You didn't lose anything; they lost.

SPEAK UP

Earlier in this book I told you to forgive yourself.
One of those reasons could be for you to find your voice.
To know that you don't have to be treated any old kind
of way.
Many of us have an issue with saying what's on our mind,
respectfully.
And when we do speak what's on our mind it can come off
as rudeness.
There is a way of saying things without offending.
Some of us can allow things to fester and think that it's all
good.
Well, it's not good at all, those annoyances can cause so
much mental disturbance.
There is no problem with speaking to people respectfully.
If there's a concern or problem that is arising.
You may think that it's inappropriate to do something
You may not be comfortable doing.
Conflicts are going to happen,
But staying silent while others say whatever is not always
okay.
You will have more of a peace of mind,
Once you find your voice to stand up for what's right.

ATTITUDES

Our approach to things can tell a lot about us.
How a person reacts when someone doesn't do what they
want them to do
Says a lot about how that person truly thinks of others.
They can choose to be angry over something that is so
small
Instead of looking at themselves to see if they're wrong.
We can overreact in times of not having things done the
way we want them to.
Immaturity is displayed because we refuse to admit our
flaws
And we can be so quick to point out others.
A lot can be seen in a person's attitude with others.
From our adulthood, attitudes are a reflection of us.
Rather good or evil, our way of doing things at a
certain age
Is not to be blamed on anybody else but ourselves.

THE 4 SEASONS

The wintertime starts a little bit before every year ends.
Most people where I'm from choose to stay inside as much
as they can
To avoid the coldness.
After the winter, people start coming outside more.
As springtime starts
Beaches get packed with people and lots of outdoor
activities happen.
The summer months are kind of like spring.
The kids are out for school, getting on their parents' nerves.
People fire up their grills to prepare for cookouts.
As soon as they get used to this time the fall will make its
way like no other.
Getting back into the swing of things seems like the hardest
part.
With the sudden change of the weather, the times seem to
go by fast for many.
And before you know it the year is almost ending, starting
everything over again.

BODY IMAGE

As soon as a person gains a pound out of their normal body weight
People will call them fat and they are constantly told that they're gaining weight.
The way some people hold being in shape to a high regard,
But being overweight as a disgrace or a mockery is unfortunate.
It can be a number of reasons why someone starts to gain weight.
After being obese for however long, some decide to get in shape.
If they lose all the weight, they're told they look better.
As a person who gained a lot of weight and was told time and time again about it
It can be irksome to be made fun of for putting on extra pounds.
I was never made fun of about my weight until I became a little obese.
And it was displeasing to hear many people make mean remarks.
Through it all I love myself.
For those that are going through the same thing, love yourself.
Your body is going to change, and you should be ok with that.
If you have good health, peace, and happiness that's more than enough.

IMPERFECT

A MIND THING

We have so many things that run through our heads daily.
Some are good and some are bad,
It can be difficult for some to shake those bad thoughts off.
We're told so many things by others
And those comments can have us thinking to act on it.
Nobody forces adults to do anything, we do things because we want to.
Many aren't strong enough to block out the badness.
The mind can lead us into believing false hope.
And simply make a fool out of ourselves.
So, if you have a thought that doesn't appear right,
You should take time out to think about it.
It could be something you don't need, something to throw you off track.
Think before you do, most importantly.

NOT BEING DEFINED

Many of us come from humble beginnings.
For those that made it out of that, hopefully you are ok.
It's very significant that wherever you come from
You don't allow the odds to come against you.
A lot of us have big dreams, in hopes that one day they will
come true.
It can be hard when you're surrounded by toxicity.
When you told those people what you wanted to do, they
laughed.
It was a slap in the face; however, it shouldn't stop you.
The environment we come from may not have been the
safest.
Making it out without compromising yourself was
something you wanted.
Even the naysayers don't have too much to say.
When they see how far you have come
You're just happy that you don't have to live like that no
more.
You beat every obstacle that came for you, and you are not
done yet.

LOOKING IN THE MIRROR

So many times, people enjoy pointing their fingers at others.
In order to keep themselves from looking a certain way.
They think that they don't do anything wrong.
People like this typically have a problem.
We all have done things that we're not too proud of.
Owning up to our mishaps takes bravery.
To stand in our setbacks without any shame is commendable.
People are so quick to call others out with ease.
While it's good to say when others are incorrect
We should have that same energy for ourselves when we do wrong.

PATIENCE

It seems like people are always in a rush.
They freak out as time continues passing by.
If others are around them, they can take some of their
anger out on them.
Usually, it's no humanity for others when some people get
like this.
"Hurry Up! Hurry Up!" is all they can say.
Some don't take a deep breath and figure out a better way
of handling situations.
A lot of moving around but hardly anything is getting done.
When things are done, they may want to give up
And not do anything else because of them being distracted.
How many of us have had times like this?
How many of us are still doing things like this?
Is handling crisis with such fury the way to go?

THE POWER OF WORDS

Some people enjoy cussing people out.
Even when at times it's not necessary to do.
The littlest things get to people, and they speak out of rage.
They may say sorry later but how many sorrys
Does it take for us to realize words do hurt?
Words can hurt a lot more than physical abuse.
When that scar heals the pain can go away.
As far as verbal abuse,
We can still have those hurtful words replay in our mind.
Nobody that I know wants to be talked down upon.
Being treated worse than a filthy animal.
Words can speak loud and not just in sound.

BEHIND THE FAÇADE

We can get into a space where a person's image is
everything.
How we dress, how we act, how we talk
Just to name a few traits that we identify with.
Some of us put so much into a perception
That we forget about our authentic selves.
To fool others, we pretend like we have it all together.
Saying things that can be untrue.
But because things behind closed doors are in shambles,
Putting on a front to please others
Seems like the way to go in order to keep up with the ideal
persona.
Every time we do that it's like we're dying on the inside.
A piece of us is not well.
Everything we see we shouldn't believe is true.
Everything isn't ok and it's ok to say that.

STRONG PEOPLE
NEED HELP TOO

Most groups have that person they consider like "the leader."

Their opinion is highly valued.

They're the go-to person when in time of need.

But when that person has a problem, who is there for them?

Others may think that person they look up to is all good

And that could be correct.

Yet and still, that strong friend or family member needs help.

It can be hard to believe that.

With them being the person that many depend on.

Strong people have their days where they need someone to talk to

Or lean on for help.

Everyone needs some type of guidance.

Some may not vocalize it but it can be determined by their behavior.

It doesn't matter how much a person appears to be tough.

We all fold here and there, while it's good to support yourself

It's just as good to have others around you to help as well.

NO FILTER

The camera strikes as you take a picture.
You look at the picture to see how you look.
You notice the discoloration in your face, your hair is a little unkempt,
You gained a few pounds, and it shows in certain areas of the picture.
You go through the filters of your phone to see if the picture can get any better.
Something in your mind tells you not to post a filter for once.
As you stare at the picture to see other imperfections
Your mind is going back and forth with posting this picture.
You think about how good others look in their pictures and then there's you.
You continue to go back and forth while posting a no filter picture
Even though you see attractive looking people on social media and in your daily life.
Finally, with no hesitation, you post the picture with you being your natural self.
No fancy filters or backgrounds, just plain ole you the way you were made.

NOT YOUR DAY

Frustration fills you as the day goes on.
You figure that today isn't the day for you.
Everything you do has gone wrong.
From the morning time where breakfast didn't come out as good,
You were late getting to the place you needed to go to.
When you walk into a room, you see the stares at you.
You didn't have enough time to get yourself ready.
Because you hit the alarm clock a couple times to get some more rest.
So, everything on you sort of look halfway decent.
Around lunchtime you tried to get things back on track and that still didn't work.
Now you just want to get in your bed and try it over again.
You think to yourself that it can't get any worse than this.
You tell people about how horrible a day you had.
And they listen with an open mind.
This day proves that not every day is going to be fine.
Tomorrow will hopefully be a lot smoother; it all depends on you.

COMPLETE

You showed me a better me.
When I was at my lowest you took my hand and picked
me up
While everyone else watched me with no help to give.
When nobody was there for me you were.
I hope you don't ever leave me because I wouldn't know
what to do.
There's no one like you that stands on everything they say.
You treat everybody fairly because you know how it is to be
mistreated.
Ever since I met you, you've never changed.
I ask you to give me more of you, and you did.
I am full now that I have you.

GETAWAY

VACATIONS ARE NECESSARY

When the world becomes a bit too much for us.
Or sometimes we just need to enjoy ourselves
To get our minds back to normal.
Going out of town for some time may be the solution.
Vacations can come at a time where we need it the most.
Rather we go with family, friends or have the courage to go
by ourselves.
Your bags have been packed.
You paid for your hotel visit.
And everything is taken care of in your household.
Now it's time to go away and leave your worries behind.
A place is calling your name and it's waiting for you to
answer.

IT DOESN'T TAKE MUCH

When going on a trip, so many people think you need a
bunch of stuff
To have the ultimate vacation.
Rather it be for one day or longer.
Some people can over pack and think nothing of it,
Allowing their bags to slow them down.
Just having the items to make it through the day is enough
already.
Some don't need a bunch of material things to satisfy
them.
They can just bring themselves and a few items and
that's it.
They're ok,
The simple things can be better than the stuff people put
on a pedestal.
We shouldn't get so wrapped up in needing a whole lot.
The necessities should make us alright.

WHAT TO DO?

Now that you're at the destination you plan on being at.
You can finally have that quality time you have been
looking for.
One thing that many people do is plan their activities.
What places should you go to?
Would you like to go shopping?
Should you go to the downtown area and sight see?
Or maybe you should stay in the hotel by yourself
And just enjoy being in another area for the time being.
Whatever it is you decide to do, it should be something you
want to do.
A getaway is for you to have peace of mind.
The family members or friends that you may have come
with
Should want the same.
Have you figured out what you're going to do on your trip?

LET'S RIDE

Buckle up, this is going to be a fun ride
As we pass by places and people we have never seen
before.
We're not going to get lost.
While outside we'll see many vehicles on the road.
Many people are out walking on the sidewalk.
Restaurants are open as you start to think of a place to go
eat at.
The eye-catching shopping stores make you want to find a
parking spot
And see what's in them the more you ride through the
areas.
You start to notice how different this town is from your
own town you live in.
You're not quite missing home right now,
With all the new entertainment that's around.
You do get out to grab a bite to eat and walk around a bit.
But then you're back in the car to see more.
Time passes on but you don't recognize it.
The day is being spent driving around seeing the different
sites.

WHAT YOU CAME FOR

You've let down your guard.
You've finally started to see that this vacation was very necessary.
You're not worried about money because this moment is more special.
As you rode through the town,
You now got a good feeling about the rest of the time.
At this point, you're midway through the trip.
All is going as planned; you didn't know what to expect once you got there.
But you start to see that you don't have any regrets
About taking some time out for yourself.
You have been so strong for others that you kind of forgotten about you.
It's no animosity, just letting the good times roll.

A GOOD NIGHT

It's been a good day so far, the sun is going down, and people are still out.
You and the people you came with are about to experience the nightlife.
There still are things to do after riding around the city.
Seeing things how they are during daytime was great.
The nighttime is good too with the city lights lighting up across town.
The bars and clubs are packed even though you don't have to go there.
Just walking down the streets with others
Being able to see this is something you had to be there to know.
A different kind of high,
You're out and about laughing, enjoying the times.
Some may say your night was wasted.
Without engaging in the usual activities that others do when they're out of town.
And that's ok, this trip is for your mind, body, and soul.

PHOTOS

One of the first things that many people do is take photos.
The reason being is for them to have something that they
can share or remember.
While on this getaway, you have taken some pictures.
You choose which one you are going to share with others.
You slowly but surely forget about the troubles you have
faced.
In the last few days, you have gone out.
And just about every time you have taken some photos.
One selfie that you took kind of show your tiredness.
Another picture shows your eagerness to see what this
journey was going to bring.
When you stepped out for a night out,
The camera flashed and caught you dressed in your finest.
These times don't last forever but with photos they can be
with you forever.

TIME FLYING BY

We all despise when time seems to drag on when hard situations are upon us.
However, whenever we are enjoying ourselves.
It appears that time goes by so fast.
You look at your watch and see it's the start of a new day.
After you get through with doing things that brings enthusiasm
The day seems like it has gone away so quickly.
It's like the day knew you were going to have a good day.
That's not really the point, the point of this is to be grateful at all times.
The time has been great for you.
And it looked as if it went by so fast.
The past is something we can never get back.
So, while we are here, let's have as much fun as possible
Live in the moment.

BITTERSWEET

The last day of your vacation is here.
You've had some of the best days of your life.
And you didn't have to do too much.
Some sightseeing and fun activities that left you smiling.
When you first got here, you didn't know what to expect.
But your expectations went above and beyond.
Unfortunately, reality is about to be back in for you.
Days of relaxing and not having any worries are kind of
coming to an end.
Fifty percent of you is not ready for you to leave.
The other fifty percent is ready for you to go back home.
And face whatever it is for you to deal with.
You enjoyed your time off and now it's back to reality.

FULLY REJUVENATED

Take a deep breath, as you leave your hotel room for the
last time.
The car ride home seems like it's longer.
You're not sad at all,
When you think about the vacation you just got off.
It was much needed, it put your mind at peace.
You got all of what you wanted.
You're now at home unpacking.
Ready to tell others about how much fun you had.
The times you had can't fully be explained.
Not because you were always inebriated.
But your spirit was lifted.
You were once down in the dumps.
And now you're on cloud nine with high hopes.

MUSIC

BACK IN THE DAYS

Many older people will say
That music back in their times was much better.
It's no secret that artists of the past differ from today's
artists.
With all the genres appearing as if they were blended all
together
The internet is one of the places
That made it seem as if anybody could be an artist.
I will admit that I listen more to the music that I grew up to
Then what's out today.
Part of that is I get a bit of nostalgia.
I constantly revert back to the 90's and 2000s rappers and
singers.
Good music is still out there, that's without a doubt,
You just must look for what you like.

THE BEAT

Before you hear a word from an artist it can be the beat
that pulls you in.
Rather it be something fast and catchy, something that
could make you tap your feet.
Or it be something smooth and melodic.
That makes you want to slowly dance with somebody.
Beats can make or break a song.
When it's done right a song can get played so much
To where others will cover or have their own rendition of it.
It's all inspiration from the originators to the ones being
influenced.
You can distinguish the genre of music someone is making.
By how the instruments are used.
Some blend genres together to make theirs standout.
Making listeners enjoy what they created when the beat
drops.

THE LYRICS

Anybody that's a songwriter can write a song,
But it takes a unique person to put together a song,
lyrically.
Beautifully putting words together that tells a story.
For the audience that understands where an artist is
coming from
Because they see a lot of them when the artists perform it.
There are so many messages in certain songs when we
listen.
That many people will never find.
For those that still read the lyrics of a song
And completely understand the true meaning of the music.
May have a song hit different for them.
A lot of artists have a story to tell in their music.
Have you been listening?

ON REPEAT

There's always a song or more than one song.
That whenever we hear it, it takes us back to that time.
It could be when we first heard it, with either good or bad memories,
The neighborhood we lived in, the people we were around and so forth and so on.
We go back and watch the video or hear the song.
And instantly get wrapped up in reminiscing over these types of records.
This could happen when we have free time or in between doing things.
But when it happens our mind gets to thinking
As the music goes on, the times oh boy the times.
There's always that one artist that speaks to us when we need it.
It's like they know who we are.
The artist can come up with good music that we can't get enough of.
Music that doesn't matter how old we get,
We will always have a connection to it making us play it again after it ends.

A SPECIAL SONG

As fans of music,
We may come across a song that speaks to us like no other.
From the beat to the lyrics to the message of a song
Gets us right where we need to be.
It's the song that gets us through some difficult times.
A song that says all we need to say when we become
speechless.
Sometimes it will leave you in tears.
Giving you the healing just from pushing play.
You know the song and every word in it.
It's more than a bop.
It's your go to when you don't know where to go.
Pick me up when you're down.
You were so busy looking for help.
And didn't have the best of luck finding that.
You listened to your special song and was good after all.

AS ONE

Venues packed with tons of fans roaring from side to side.
Ready to see their favorite artists put on a show like no other.
The lights turned down and the stage has been set on fire
By the performer's electrifying set.
This is what the concert goers paid their money for.
Many had counted down the days, took time off, and waited patiently.
For them all to be under one roof enjoying themselves.
After the concert, their feet are a little tired from all that standing.
And they have lost a bit of their voice.
They saw the best concert of their life.
The crowd was hypnotized through the lively music that sounded great everywhere.

HIP-HOP

It didn't take me too long to get into rap music.
Although many have a strong dislike for it,
I can never recall a time were hip-hop completely turned
me off.
Many of the stories I can't relate to, but I understand.
The honesty, the bravery to be so open with a possible past
time.
Putting rhymes together that make millions recite along.
A catchy hook is always great.
What was once a new song turns into a classic years later.
Inspiring a new generation after the pioneers
Laid their foundations for others to be inspired.
The movement of the culture is undeniable.
Many have slept on the genre but now have no other choice
but to be awakened by it.
The music won't ever stop being made.
The journey continues as rappers have new avenues.

R&B

There's something oh so special about Rhythm & Blues.
R&B is short for Rhythm & Blues for those that don't know.
It can be slow or fast.
As long as it's pleasing to the ears,
Many people will say that back in the day R&B and music
overall was better.
And they may have a point when listening to what's the
wave now.
There are still currently some good singers.
Rather you're a big fan of today's music.
People still haven't stopped listening.
It's certain music that makes me close my eyes
And envision that I am somewhere else other than home.
The soul, the style, the honest storytelling, and more of
R&B songs
Have kept me around wanting more.

A LOT OF FIRSTS

There have been many firsts for many of us that included a song being played.

It's crazy how we incorporate music into major events that happens to us.

Sometimes it's not even played, it's just the way things happen.

Music can set a tone for what's about to come next.

It tells what's going on, not too overpowering.

But just enough to capture the moment.

A song playing in the background can be all that you need.

You can remember this after you finish the enjoyment.

The song or songs that was played can take a moment up a notch.

MUSIC LOVER

Ever since I was a little boy, music has been a part of me.
I was once and kind of still am, an outcast.
When I didn't know who to go to, listening to music was
my safety place.
I could turn on a song and that could shift my whole mood.
There's not a day that goes by that I don't hear some type
of song.
It can be a slow jam, mid-tempo, or upbeat song that I
become absorbed in.
I'm a true music lover that can get into different sub-genres
That many might not particularly like.
Ever since YouTube has come into existence
I have watched tons of video clips of some artist's
performances,
Music videos and the behind the scenes look.
I can go from the 90's, to the 2000's, to the 2010's up
until now.
Music has me mesmerized and I can't fully let go of it.

LOVE

LOVE IS GREAT

It's what most people want.
That one person that takes them away to endless warmth.
To have someone that they can go to no matter what.
For those that understand the real meaning behind love,
knows this.
They waited and had their fair share of ups and downs.
Now they're up and there's no coming down.
Waiting for that moment to have the love of their life.
Many lessons were taught to them.
And they finally see what it is.
To have a person to hold them down through thick and
thin.
It didn't take a wedding ring to prove that their bond is
strong.
Just by them staying true to each other was enough.
Everyday genuine love is given.

ARE YOU READY?

You can put on a front about how much in love you're in.
People say they're in need of love,
But don't know what to do when a person shows them love.
It takes more than material things and expensive trips
To prove how much you care about someone.
You can say things to make it appear
As if you're ok with sharing your world.
However, that façade we put on can only last for so long.
So, when you say you're ready to have that special person
to be with,
How sure are you?
Because when it comes to playing with someone's heart
The joke can be back on you.
Leaving you stuck with questions about yourself.
Were you ready for love or were you just dreaming?

A SAFE PLACE

So much goes on through the day that you can't wait to get home
And be in the arms of the person that you adore.
They don't criticize you or make you think twice about yourself.
They don't have to say much.
They can look at you and see you're in need of affection.
The time has come for you to get what you want.
They hold you tight, rub your back, and tell you everything is going to be ok.
It doesn't take long for you to be put back at ease.
It's nice to know that you have a person you can go to in this time of need.
The care and compassion they have for you
Can't be replaced by no other human being.
Even when you let them go, you still empathize with them.
They never will leave you, in their arms is where you go as much as possible.

BEDROOM

To start things off, I kiss you passionately to set the mood
off right.
Rubbing all over your body.
You hold me, allowing me to get deep inside.
This is the ride of a lifetime, action packed.
It's like magic.
Tears fall down your eyes because of amazing gratification.
My knees start to get weak when I get ready for the big
climax.
We're happy.
The anticipation of wanting to see you again afterwards.
So, we can experience that same feeling over,
Is always on my mind, how about you?

STAY THE SAME

When people are in a relationship many try to switch up
the flow of things.
While change is good, it's not needed with everything.
You can start to notice a person changing by their behavior.
It's a number of reasons why people get like this.
If you're truly in love with someone
There's not a lot of fixing that should take place.
Allowing the wrong things to tempt you.
In a relationship could destroy what you have already built.
It takes a strong-minded person
To not be influenced by things that are used to create
badness.
Changing on someone isn't always good.
When it's only for your advantage.
You don't have to become a different person as time
goes on,
If you're a good person then they will love you just the way
they met you.

OPINIONS, COMMENTS, AND REPLIES

People are going to talk about relationships others have.
Some of what they say could be true and some not.
The one thing that couples shouldn't play into
Is allowing the misjudgments of others.
Take away what you have built together.
How you respond to the stories can also determine
Will you allow the ideas from someone else to break what you have?
Making something that could be so special be so wrong on your part.
Don't be that person to believe the hype
More than you believe your supposed lover.
Whatever you choose to do
Don't allow the wrong people to invade something that is true with lies.

VALENTINE'S DAY

February 14th is the day for couples to show their love.
No relationship is perfect but for this day.
It should be as close to being perfect as it can.
This day is made to show each other admiration.
To remind someone they love even after being together for some time.
It's more than just receiving gifts.
Nice gifts are fine and dandy.
But the fact that you have each other is what matters.
Knowing what it takes to make that person smile.
And keeping that smile there.
If you're truly in love
Don't let February 14th be the only day for you to show how much you care.
Allow it to be a prelude to how things will always be.

RESPECT

Respect is a word that many want.
Some don't even give it but expect others to give them that.
It's like at times, people can be so invested in a person.
That they give up themselves to please them.
We all have our way of thinking
But some things should be simple to understand.
We can say a lot of things to make it appear one way.
But we know deep down the truth.
Having the courage to stand strong in what's right
Is what many of us were taught to do.
To make the person we love free of pain from our actions.
So that another relationship won't go down the drain.
Respect is something that we shouldn't always have to tell others.
It should be given to us if you act in a manner that shows just that.

DISBELIEF

So many questions run through your head.
While being betrayed by a person you're in love with.
You can't believe they would do such a thing to you.
The time and effort it took to build something solid
Has now been broken into pieces on the floor waiting for you to pick it up.
For those that have been there before, you have probably had enough.
The strength to walk away and never come back seems kind of hard for you to do.
Not wanting to be alone when you get home.
Is something you wouldn't dare to dream of.
It's all up to you to make that decision on staying or going.
This is not only for women but for us men too
Because both genders can do wrong.
You're shocked but it won't be forever.
As you move forward with or without that person.

WORTH IT

Love is something we all deserve.
It could be through friendship, family, or a relationship.
Our lives should be filled with joy.
The joy should come from us and others should be adding on to that.
It doesn't take a rocket scientist to distinguish a good person from a bad person.
Many relationships have come and go due to unforeseen circumstances.
For those that are looking for that person to add more greatness to you.
You can find that someone at the right time.
If you give up, you will never know what was in store for you.
No matter how much we put up with this image of being unfazed
We all want someone to love us for who we are.
So never give up on finding that person that will be a perfect fit for you.
Your past was there to help you get ready for what's about to come.

LOYALTY

NOT EVERYBODY

Everybody that you meet isn't going to be your friend.
We can learn that the hard way by not taking people for
who they are.
Lines can be drawn; someone can see that.
And walk right through them as if they don't know.
Leaving you confused about what you did to deserve such
treatment.
Only you can protect yourself from the wrong people.
After learning about how some people move
You now know that honesty doesn't lie in everybody.
But for those that are good people, you will know them.
You will know them as time goes on and they never switch
on you.
The days will change but they never will.
To have a strong bond amongst others is something that
some people don't have.
But when you do have that cherish it, everybody is not like
that.

FINDING GENUINE PEOPLE

If you know many people
Then you probably have been disrespected by some.
It's not shocking to think some aren't who they say
they are.
Even though you may have been used by some people.
There are still people out there that have good intentions
And can make up for those setbacks you had in the past.
When having someone new around you
It's common to not want to repeat the mistakes you made
with others.
It's never ok to judge new people by your troubled past.
They're not them, it's good to protect yourself from harm.
But not allowing someone to show you they're a good
person
Could only damage you from having someone good
around you.
There are still people that are true to self.
And if you're looking for them,
Let them come to you in their truest form.

LESS GUARDED

As you start to enjoy the company of others.
You may think that you can be more of yourself around them.
Free from judgments.
We all have certain things about us that make us different.
Many of us don't use that word friend loosely.
But after spending some time with them
You can now call them a friend.
You call and text them on a regular basis.
Tell them what type of day you had.
They may remind you of yourself; they understand you.
As time goes on, they become apart of your circle.
Your circle grew some but not too much.
Because you the type of person that doesn't allow everyone to be your friend.
You're cool with the friendships you have made.
The bad vibes are off you and the pleasant times are here to stay.

WORD IS BOND

Having a genuine person around is always good.
In times of difficulties, you can turn to them to get a better understanding.
I believe these types of people are placed in our lives
Not just for a little while but for as long as we're fortunate to have them.
We can become bullheaded without wanting to tell people things
That they could help us with.
It could be that we don't want to bother them or some other reason.
But when things get too heavy for us to carry
It's a good thing to turn to those people to get the help we need.
It could be a simple phone call to make us think more clearly.
Whenever we want to give up on something
The people that we call friends or family could be the people we may need.
Their word is solid, their word is trustworthy, their word is bond.

HONEST CONVERSATIONS

It's the type of talk that many of us try avoiding.
When we go too far left, people that love us.
Is going to reach for us to come back to our senses.
Even as adults, we can make a fool out of ourselves with
our mindsets.
Not wanting to listen is human nature for us to do
When told things for our betterment.
But it's needed, having those types of people around us
To steer us in a direction that can help than disrupt is
necessary.
It's good to have those conversations on the phone.
For some, to get through to someone in a more
efficient way
A face-to-face conversation could be the way to go.
Seeing each other facial expressions
And shake hands afterwards to let them know it's all love.
It's never hate when telling someone something
To prevent or help them from self-destruction.

IN THE TIME OF NEED

Anytime you find yourself in trouble
The individual you go to for help.
Will be right there to help, no questions asked.
Even when you are doing well and show no signs of
badness.
They will always tell you in a comforting voice.
That they are here for you.
They saw you at your worst.
And could have left you there hopeless.
But made you hopeful to see a better you.
No gift could ever replace what they had done for you.
They didn't do it out of sorrowness,
It was something placed in them to do.

WHAT ABOUT YOU?

It's a good thing for people to show acts of kindness.
Some get so used to others doing for them,
But is that same generosity being returned back?
It's not about if someone does something for you.
You must do something back for them to one up.
A favor should never be forced
It should be something we're willing to do when that time comes.
When it comes to friends, family members, and associates
If they have been nice to you, then it's a no brainer for you to do the same.
Have that 50/50 relationship with all of those around you.
Stay mindful of how you treat others.
It's good to receive from people
But also give back to others whenever it's necessary.

NEVER

A loyal person has qualities about them that will forever be shown.
Being around a loyal person can teach someone.
That may not have the same characteristics as them.
Loyalty never changes.
As a loyal person, you would never have to question them about their actions.
If you are a person with morals, you would never take from them.
You would never betray them
You would never do something that's completely disrespectful to them.
And not apologize and know not to do that again.
You would never take that person for granted.
Loyalty is something that some just don't have.
Some will be friends with you today
And tomorrow act like they never met you.
A loyal person may have been done wrong.
But as many times as they have been wrong, they never change.

IT BE LIKE THAT

In a friendship, there will be times
Where you may not agree with someone.
We all have our own minds to think.
And at times, we don't do everything alike.
All friendships will go through a time when
You may not speak as much as you used to.
It could be because you're spending time doing things that
doesn't involve them,
You want some time alone or some other reason.
However long it may take for friends to reconnect with one
another.
True friendships are so strong that nothing can break them.
If people are meant to be in each other's lives, then
everything will be ok.

THANK YOU

For those that have a heart to do greatness
I just want to say your consistent greatness will not go unnoticed.
We live in a society that honors mostly things that are fake.
People get credit for not really doing anything.
And leave the ones that have done most of the work
In the back sometimes never to be seen.
Every time someone that means good gets knocked down, they choose to get up.
They rise to dust themselves off, not being disturbed by the stumbling block.
Your fearless and selfless, all values that a strong person should have.
You do things out of realness, not for recognition.
But for those that see what you do, may not have those attributes.
They can watch and admire the bravery.
And one day, maybe, they'll have that same boldness.

AUTHOR'S NOTE

The goal for *Living...* is to not only show off my writing range but also give my personal thoughts on various subjects. As I wrote my notes before writing this book, I had an idea for why I wrote *Living...*; however, after working with my book editor and publishing assistant, my mind opened up to me not just having a book to publish, but having my own voice so my projects can stand out amongst the rest.

There are many experiences within these poems that relate to my life personally. At first, I was kind of nervous to put some of my past and even present moments in this book. But the more I grow, the more I am allowing myself to step out of my comfort zone and go for what I truly want. The overall theme for this book is human nature and, yes, I guarantee there is a poem for everyone. The writing process was extremely easy for me because I have read some poems, and I knew this was a good challenge for me to take on. My mood was calm while writing this book, I do have other books I have written, but because those books were written from a dark space, I wanted to try something new, something more fun.

My hope for this book is to send good vibrations to the world, allowing my message to be loud and clear for audiences that want to hear it. I don't want this to be my last book, but while I have this chance with my first published book, I want my work to be as authentic as possible. The poems, for me, are like a steady flow; there are ups and downs just like everyday living.

Thank you for reading *Living* …
If you enjoyed this book,
please help spread the word by
leaving an online review.

www.ingramcontent.com/pod-product-compliance
Lightning Source LLC
Chambersburg PA
CBHW030313130626
46549CB00002B/841